Morris Mouse

One day, Miss Price
came to school with a box.

The box had a blue ribbon.
On the ribbon
was a birthday card.

Inside the box was a mouse.

Miss Price found a cage
in the storeroom.
When the children
came to school,
the mouse was
in its new home.

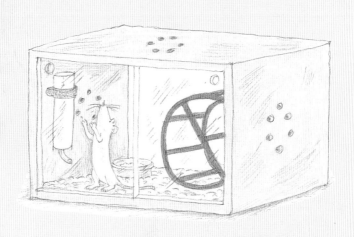

The children liked the mouse.
They let him sit
on their hands
and run up their arms.

They watched him
wash his whiskers
and eat bits of apple.

Every day, the children
cleaned the mouse cage.
One child held the mouse.
One child cleaned out the cage.
One child got fresh water,
and one child got fresh food.

Miss Price made a chart
to show whose turn it was.

Who Will Clean the Mouse Cage?	
Monday	Simon, Danny, Amy
Tuesday	Jack, Jared, Sara
Wednesday	Becky, Laura, Ali
Thursday	Kris, Lisa, Sami
Friday	Jade, Zac, Tyson

One day, some children measured the mouse. Other children wrote mouse poems.

11

Some children went
to the school library
to find out about mice.

They made a chart
about mice.

Soon the room was full
of graphs, posters, and poems,
but the little mouse
still had no name.

Miss Price asked everyone
to write a name on paper.
She put all the names
in a box, then she asked
Mr Cook to take out a name.
He took out the name
Morris.

15

The children loved Morris.
They looked after him well.

They took turns taking him
home for the weekend.